animal planet™

I Am an
Incredible Animal

Silver Dolphin

P1 PRE-LEVEL 1: ASPIRING READERS

1 LEVEL 1: EARLY READERS

2 LEVEL 2: DEVELOPING READERS

- Simple factual texts with mostly familiar themes and content
- Concepts in text are supported by images
- Includes glossary to reinforce reading comprehension
- Repetition of basic sentence structure with variation of placement of subjects, verbs, and adjectives
- Introduction to new phonic structures
- Integration of contractions, possessives, compound sentences, and some three-syllable words
- Mostly easy vocabulary familiar to kindergarteners and first-graders

3 LEVEL 3: ENGAGED READERS

4 LEVEL 4: FLUENT READERS

Silver Dolphin Books
An imprint of Printers Row Publishing Group
A division of Readerlink Distribution Services, LLC
9717 Pacific Heights Blvd, San Diego, CA 92121
www.silverdolphinbooks.com

© 2021 Discovery or its subsidiaries and affiliates. Animal Planet and related logos are trademarks of Discovery or its subsidiaries and affiliates, used under license. All rights reserved. AnimalPlanet.com

Printers Row Publishing Group is a division of Readerlink Distribution Services, LLC.
Silver Dolphin Books is a registered trademark of Readerlink Distribution Services, LLC.

Written by Lori C. Froeb
Designed by Andrew Barthelmes

All notations of errors or omissions should be addressed to Silver Dolphin Books, Editorial Department, at the above address.

ISBN: 978-1-64517-523-0
Manufactured, printed, and assembled in Heshan, China.
First printing, December 2021. LP/12/21
25 24 23 22 21 1 2 3 4 5

All photography © iStock/Getty Images except for the following images: Pascal Deynat/Odontobase p. 18T; PARFENOV1976 p. 108B.

CONTENTS

A NOTE TO PARENTS

Learning to read is an exciting time in your child's life! This book will help aspiring readers get started on their journeys.

All-Star Readers were created to help make learning to read a fun and engaging experience. Carefully selected stories and subject matter support the acquisition of reading skills, encourage children to learn about the world around them, and help develop a life-long love of books.

This Animal Planet Level 2 collection offers fascinating factual content that is carefully crafted for developing readers. Every child is unique, and age or grade level does not determine a particular reading level. See the previous page for a description of the reading level in this book.

As you read with your child, read for short periods of time and pause often. Encourage her to sound out words she does not know. Suggest she look at the picture on the page for clues about what the word might be. Have younger children turn the pages and point to pictures and familiar words. Each story in this book includes a glossary that defines new vocabulary words. When your child comes across a boldfaced word she doesn't recognize, instruct her to turn to the glossary and read its definition.

A good way to reinforce reading comprehension is to have a conversation about the book after finishing it. Children love talking about their favorite parts! As your child becomes a more independent reader, encourage him to discuss ideas and questions he may have.

Remember that there is no right or wrong way to share books with your child. When you find time to read with your child, you create a pattern of enjoying and exploring books that will become a love of reading!

I Am a
SHARK

I am a shark. There are over four hundred species of sharks on Earth.

I am a great white shark. I am the largest **predator** in the ocean!

Sharks have been around for a long time.

We have been around for more than four hundred million years!

My biggest **ancestor** was megalodon.

Scientists believe megalodon grew up to sixty feet long.

That's longer than a school bus!

Here is a megalodon tooth next to one of my teeth.

Many scientists believe megalodon was the largest fish to ever live.

Great white sharks are probably the most famous sharks.

We have even been in many movies!

But sharks come in many shapes and sizes.

plankton

This is a whale shark. She is the biggest fish in the world!

She may be big, but she eats tiny creatures called **plankton**.

This is a hammerhead.

His head shape lets him see **prey** better than other sharks.

He also uses his head to catch food. He pins down prey in the sand, and then eats it.

This is a zebra shark.

She has spots now, but when she was born she had stripes like a zebra.

The zebra shark spends most of her time on the ocean floor.

This is a thresher shark. Check out that long tail.

The thresher uses his tail to stun fish by slapping them.

Sharks come in different shapes and sizes, but we have many things in common.

All sharks are fish. All sharks are cold-blooded.

Our bodies are the same temperature as the water around us.

Sharks don't have bones. Instead, our skeletons are made out of **cartilage**.

Cartilage is flexible and light.

It makes it easier to swim faster and longer.

Every shark has these basic parts:

nose

Sharks have an amazing sense of smell.

eyes

Sharks have eyes, but no eyelids.

gill slits

Sharks can have five, six, or seven gill slits on each side.

jaws

The jaws can move forward to grab prey. Most animal jaws only move up and down.

pectoral fins

These fins help the shark move up and down.

caudal fin

This tail fin moves back and forth to make the shark move forward.

dorsal fins

These fins keep the shark from rolling over.

pelvic fins

These fins help the shark steer and stop.

We have scales like other fish.

Our scales are called **dermal denticles**. Denticle means "little tooth."

The denticles make shark skin feel like sandpaper.

They make water move over our bodies faster.

To pick up speed, we use our tail fins.

Every species of shark has a different-shaped tail fin.

We move our tail fins back and forth to go forward.

great white shark

blacktip reef shark

hammerhead shark

thresher shark

All sharks have sharp teeth—lots of them!

This is a good thing because our teeth fall out often.

tiger shark

great white shark

bull shark

mako shark

oceanic whitetip shark

When one tooth falls out, another moves into its place.

A great white can have three hundred teeth in its jaws at one time.

During my lifetime, I may go through thirty thousand teeth.

Adult humans only have thirty-two teeth. If one falls out, it is not replaced.

Most sharks are born alive, but some hatch from egg cases.

A catshark laid these egg cases.

Baby sharks are called pups.

You can see the pups growing inside.

adult catshark

Shark pups that are born alive have an extra challenge.

They must swim away quickly or their mother may eat them!

Great whites like me hang out in the shallow parts of oceans all around the world.

We like the warmer water that is found there.

But we also travel to deeper water and further out to sea.

Usually, I follow my nose to where the food is!

Sharks have an amazing sense of smell.

We can sniff tiny amounts of blood in the water to find prey.

My nose will even tell me which direction the scent is coming from.

Take a close look at my nose.

See those small dots?

They are organs that can feel electrical fields in the water.

Sharks can detect a fish's heartbeat if it is nearby.

Like all sharks, I am a **carnivore**. This means I eat meat.

Here are some of my favorite foods:

dolphins

sea lions

sea turtles

rays

tuna

Sometimes other sharks!

We do not hunt humans for food.

Sometimes we attack a human by mistake.

Our only predators are humans.

They kill more than one hundred million of us a year.

My belly is white and my back is dark gray.

I am hard to see in the deep water from above.

I am also hard to see in the sunlit water from below.

This is called **countershading**.

I can surprise my prey
because it doesn't see me.

I can surprise my prey another way.

I **breach** to hunt seals near the surface.

To breach, I swim up fast from below the seal.

I am so fast that I fly into the air after grabbing the seal.

I splash back into the water and enjoy my meal.

Great whites are one of the only shark species that do this.

All this talk about hunting has made me hungry!

I am going to go grab something to eat.

See you later!

Super Shark Stats!

Fastest

A mako shark can swim sixty miles per hour.
That is as fast as a car on the highway!

Toothiest

A bull shark can have three hundred and fifty teeth
in its mouth at one time.

Biggest

A whale shark can weigh as much as four elephants.

Hardest to Spot

A wobbegong shark uses **camouflage** to blend in with the seafloor. Can you find it?

Glossary

ancestor: a relative that lived in the past

breach: to swim upward fast enough to leave the water

camouflage: an animal's coloring that helps it hide and blend in

carnivore: an animal that eats meat

cartilage: a light, rubbery material from which a shark's skeleton is made

countershading: a type of camouflage where the bottom of the body is light and the top is dark

dermal denticles: tiny toothlike scales covering a shark's skin

plankton: tiny animals that float near the ocean's surface

predator: an animal that hunts other animals for food

prey: an animal that is hunted by other animals for food

I Am a
POLAR
BEAR

Hi there! Welcome to my chilly home.

I am a polar bear, and these are my cubs.

We do not see humans very often.

We live far from any cities or towns.

All polar bears live in the Arctic.

The Arctic is the northernmost part of Earth.

Winters are long, dark, and cold in the Arctic.

Summers are short and cool.

Polar bears live in Russia, Norway, Greenland, Canada, and Alaska in the United States.

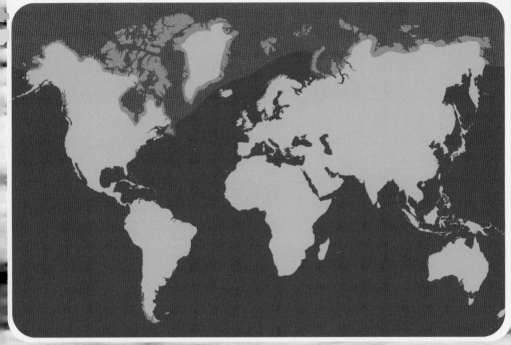

The Arctic is covered by snow and ice for most of the year.

The temperature can drop to minus fifty degrees in winter.

But I am not cold.

Polar bears are covered with very thick fur.

My fur looks white, but each strand of hair is clear.

My fur is very warm and good **camouflage**.

I am hard to spot if I am laying still in the snow.

Under all this fur, my skin is black.

The black color absorbs the sun's light and warms me up!

My body has another way of staying warm: **blubber**!

Blubber is fat. I have a layer of blubber under my skin.

It is four inches thick in places.

The blubber keeps me warm when I swim in the icy water.

Polar bears are great at swimming!

We can swim for days if we need to.

Look at my front paws. They are as big as dinner plates.

I use my front paws like giant paddles in the water.

My paws are great for walking on the snow and ice, too.

The bottoms are covered in tiny bumps.

The bumps grip the slippery ice.

Polar bears are **marine mammals**.

The ocean provides us with food and a place to live.

Dolphins, sea otters, and seals are also marine mammals.

sea otter

polar bear

dolphin

bearded seal

Seals are our favorite food!

Polar bears are the largest **predators** on land.

Male bears can weigh as much as ten adult humans.

Females like me are much smaller.

Polar bears spend most of their lives floating on **sea ice**.

Sea ice is frozen ocean water.

I jump onto floating pieces of ice to travel.

I also use the floating ice as resting places when I'm swimming.

I use the sea ice for something else—hunting seals.

Seals come to holes in the ice to breathe.

I can smell a seal's breathing hole from a mile away.

I follow my nose to the hole.

Then I wait quietly and watch the hole.

When a seal pops out of the hole to breathe, I quickly grab it.

My cubs learn how to hunt from watching me.

The sea ice is around from fall to spring.

We eat as many seals as we can.

The seals' blubber makes us fat.

When the sea ice melts in the summer, we move to shore.

There is not much to eat until the ice returns in the fall.

Sometimes a whale **carcass** washes up on the beach.

We eat its blubber and share with other polar bears.

This carcass was a lucky find.

Sometimes a hungry polar bear may hunt a musk ox or reindeer.

Some polar bears will eat seaweed or birds.

None of these things are as good for us as seals.

Many of us eat nothing for months.

We live off our fat until fall.

Earth is warming up and it is taking longer for sea ice to form.

We are spending more time on land.

It is getting harder to find food.

For this reason, polar bears are **vulnerable**.

This means our numbers are getting smaller.

If we do not find a way to survive, we will be **endangered**.

My cubs are strong.

I take good care of them.

I ate a lot of food in the spring before they were born.

I gained more than four hundred pounds!

In the fall, I dug a den in the snow.

I went into the den and rested.

Polar bears don't **hibernate** like other bears.

I did not move much and did not eat for seven months.

Polar bears usually have one, two, or three cubs.

I had two. Twins!

They were born in winter with their eyes closed.

They each weighed less than two pounds.

That is about as much as a small rabbit.

They drank my milk and grew quickly.

In the spring, we left the den.

The cubs learned to walk, swim, and play.

I finally got something to eat.

Now the cubs watch me hunt on the sea ice.

I smell a seal nearby. It is time for the cubs' lesson.

See you later!

Polar Bear Fact File

Polar bears roll in the snow to clean themselves. Clean fur is warmer than dirty fur.

Polar bears are more likely to be too hot than too cold. A quick swim cools them down.

Almost sixty percent of polar bears live in Canada. That is about sixteen thousand polar bears.

Polar bears are not hunted by any other animals. Humans are polar bears' only predator.

Glossary

blubber: a layer of fat that marine animals use for warmth and energy

camouflage: an animal's coloring that helps it hide and blend in

carcass: a dead body, usually of an animal

endangered: almost none left in the world

hibernate: to go into a deep sleep for the winter. Animals don't eat or drink while hibernating

marine mammals: mammals that depend on the ocean to live

predator: an animal that hunts other animals for food

sea ice: frozen ocean water

vulnerable: a species that will become endangered if its habitat keeps shrinking

I Am a
GORILLA

Hello! Welcome to Africa.

I am a gorilla.

There are two **species** of gorillas.

Western gorillas live in rain forests and marshes in western Africa.

They live in Cameroon, Gabon, and a few other countries.

western gorilla

AFRICA

eastern gorilla

Eastern gorillas live in mountain forests in parts of central Africa.

They are found in Rwanda, Uganda, and the Congo.

I am an eastern gorilla.

Gorillas are great apes.

Bonobos, orangutans, and chimpanzees are also great apes.

Apes do not have tails like monkeys do.

gorilla
largest of the apes

bonobo
most peaceful of the apes

Monkey, not an ape!

Monkeys have tails. Apes do not.

orangutan

spends most of its life in trees

chimpanzee

closest relative to humans

Most apes live in Africa, just like me!

Orangutans live in Asia.

Look at me. Do you think you and I look a little alike?

Humans, gorillas, and all apes are **primates**.

Monkeys are primates, too.

Primates have big brains and eyes that face forward.

Primates also have long fingers and toes.

Most primates have **opposable thumbs**.

This means we can use our thumbs to grasp things.

Humans and gorillas share more than ninety-six percent of their DNA.

DNA is what makes us what we are. It is in all our cells.

No wonder we look a little alike!

You are part of a family. I am part of a family, too.

My mom and I are part of a **troop**. A troop is a group of gorillas.

We do everything together.

My dad is in charge of the troop. He is a silverback.

The hair on his back turned silver when he became a teenager.

When I get older, I will be a silverback, too.

Dad makes sure our troop is safe.

He decides where we look for food.

If there is a fight in the troop, Dad breaks it up.

Gorillas are peaceful apes.

Most times there are no fights.

But Dad is always on the lookout for trouble.

If he sees a male gorilla he does not know, he may roar.

Sometimes he will beat his chest.

The other gorilla knows this means, "I am in charge."

Gorillas do not have many **predators**.

But our numbers in the wild are shrinking.

Humans are the biggest danger to gorillas.

Humans hunt and capture gorillas.

They also destroy gorilla **habitats**.

Today, all gorillas are **endangered**.

Gorillas use twenty-five sounds to **communicate**.

We can scream if we are angry or scared.

We hum when we eat.

A hum means we are happy.

A mother gorilla can make a grunting sound like a pig.

She uses this to tell her baby he is doing something wrong.

All gorillas walk using their knuckles and legs.

This would be very hard for you to do.

It is easy for us.

Our arms are very strong and much longer than our legs.

We can stand and walk on our feet, too.

This is helpful when we are carrying food.

Speaking of food, it is time to look for some with my troop.

Eastern gorillas are **herbivores**.

We **forage** for many hours every day.

We spend all morning looking for food. Then we nap.

When we wake up, we forage for the rest of the day.

Western gorillas are also mainly herbivores.

Fruit is easy to find in their forest, so they eat a lot of it.

They eat more than one hundred different kinds of fruit!

If fruit is hard to find, these gorillas eat leaves and bark.

Some also like to eat ants and termites.

ant

bark

leaves

termite

A hungry western gorilla may look for a termite nest.

He breaks the nest to get at the juicy termites inside.

All this foraging and eating has made me sleepy.

My troop gets ready to nap by building nests.

Mom finds branches and leaves.

She makes a nest for us on the ground.

We make a new nest every time we sleep.

I am learning how to make a nest from my mom.

After naptime, I like to play with my friends.

We climb trees, swing from branches, and wrestle.

Sometimes we even play tag!

Gorillas learn from playing.

We learn how to get along with others in our group.

We also learn how to use our arms to swing.

My friends are calling me to play right now.

See you later!

Gorillas Are Great!

An adult gorilla can eat sixty pounds of food a day!

A baby gorilla can ride on its mother's back when it is four months old. It holds on tightly.

A gorilla nose print is like a human fingerprint. No two are exactly alike!

Gorillas get the water they need from plants they eat.

Glossary

communicate: to share information, ideas, and feelings

endangered: almost none left in the world

forage: to look around for food

habitat: the place where an animal lives

herbivore: an animal that eats only plants

opposable thumbs: thumbs that can be used to grasp and hold things

predators: animals that hunt other animals for food

primate: a type of animal that has hands that can grasp things, forward-facing eyes, and large brains for their size

species: a group of living things different from all other groups

troop: a group of gorillas

I Am a
DOLPHIN

Hello, there! Welcome to my watery home.

I am a dolphin and I love to play.

I hear my friends calling me.

Would you like to meet them?

Follow me!

I live in a group of dolphins called a **pod**.

We play, hunt, and protect each other.

It is safer to stay in a group than to swim alone.

We **communicate** with clicks, squeaks, and whistles.

Every dolphin has his or her own special whistle.

All the other members of the pod know me by my whistle.

It is like having a name.

You may think dolphins are fish.
It is true that we live in the ocean, have fins, and swim.

But we are not fish.
We are mammals just like bears, gorillas, and you!

This means we are **warm-blooded** and breathe air.

We drink milk from our mothers when we are babies.

We also have hair, but only when we are first born.

Dolphins are related to whales and porpoises.

We look most like porpoises, but our noses are usually longer.

humpback whale

beluga whale
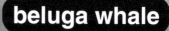

porpoise

Our closest living relative does not swim in the ocean.

It is the hippo and it lives in Africa.

Hippos spend lots of time in lakes and rivers.

There are about thirty-eight other **species** of dolphin.

Most live in the ocean.

Some live in rivers.

Atlantic spotted dolphin

dusky dolphin

short-beaked common dolphin

spinner dolphin

I am a bottlenose dolphin.

I get my name from the shape of my **rostrum**.

My species lives in the warm parts of the ocean.

We do not like the cold waters of the Arctic or Antarctic.

Many dolphins are gray, but some are pink!

This is an Amazon river dolphin.

When they are born, these dolphins are gray.

They turn pink as they get older.

The largest dolphins in the world are orcas.

They are sometimes called killer whales.

Orcas are **apex predators**.

No animals hunt orcas.

Do you see the hole in my head?

That is my blowhole.

All dolphins have one.

I breathe only through my blowhole and not through my mouth.

My blowhole is closed when I am
underwater.

When I need to take a breath,
I must come to the surface.

My blowhole opens and I take
a breath.

I also use it to make whistles
and clicks!

My pod is hungry. We will hunt for food together.

We like to eat small fish and squid.

Sometimes we eat crabs or shrimp!

Big dolphins like orcas hunt for seals.

Orcas sometimes hunt in groups. Together they can catch and eat giant whales.

Sometimes they hunt sharks!

I hear some fish nearby.

I can't see them, but I know they are there.
How?

I send a sound into the water.

The sound bounces off objects and back to me.

I can tell what and where the objects are.

This is called **echolocation**.
There is a school of fish nearby!

Dolphin pods work together to catch fish.

Sometimes a pod herds a school of fish into a large ball.

Each dolphin takes a turn swimming through the ball.

We catch and eat the fish as we swim through.

Some dolphins trap fish by mud ring feeding.

They swim in a circle to make a ring of mud in the water.

The fish jump out of the water to escape the mud, and the dolphins grab them!

Dolphins can have hundreds of teeth, but we do not chew.

We mostly use our teeth to grab **prey**.

We swallow our food whole—headfirst.

After lunch, it is playtime!

Young dolphins and adult dolphins both love to play.

We flip and spin and surf the waves.

Sometimes we will race a passing boat.

Sometimes we play catch or tug-of-war with each other.

We use whatever we can find: seaweed, sponges, or coral.

Some of us even make bubble rings for fun.

Sometimes we jump out of the water to play.

Other times we do it to get around faster and easier.

Gliding through the air takes less energy than swimming through water.

Dolphins use their **flukes** to push themselves out of the water as they swim forward.

This is called **porpoising**, and it makes traveling a breeze!

Dolphins are curious and smart.

Some of us have been trained to help find lost humans.

We know humans need air to breathe.

We help them keep their heads above water.

I hope you liked meeting my pod.
We are going to look for some waves.
It is time to play! Good-bye for now!

Dolphin Fact File

Dolphins usually have one baby at a time. The baby stays with its mother for three to six years.

A dolphin can hold its breath for about ten minutes. Some kinds of dolphin can dive 150 feet or more.

Dolphins have two stomachs. One stomach stores the food. The other stomach digests it.

An orca can grow to be almost as long as a school bus. Some orcas can weigh as much as an elephant!

Glossary

apex predator: an animal that hunts other animals, but is not hunted itself

communicate: to share information, ideas, and feelings

echolocation: using sound to see objects

fluke: a dolphin's tail fin

pod: a group of dolphins, porpoises, or whales

porpoising: to jump out of the water while swimming

prey: an animal that is hunted by other animals for food

rostrum: a dolphin's snout

species: a group of living things different from all other groups

warm-blooded: able to keep the body warm even in cold weather